Published by Christian Art Publishers,
PO Box 1599, Vereeniging, 1930, RSA

© 2014

Designed by Christian Art Publishers

Images used under license from Shutterstock.com

ISBN 978-1-4321-1252-3

Printed in China

20 21 22 23 24 25 26 27 28 – 14 13 12 11 10 9 8 7 6 5

Hope

CHRISTIAN ART
PUBLISHERS

Be strong
and take heart,
all you who hope
in the LORD.

Psalm 31:24

God is the only
One who can make
the valley of trouble
a door of hope.

Catherine Marshall

Be joyful in hope,
patient in affliction,
faithful in prayer.

Romans 12:12

He that lives
in hope dances
without music.

George Herbert

We have this
hope as an anchor
for the soul, firm and
secure. It enters the
inner sanctuary,
where our forerunner,
Jesus, has entered
on our behalf.

Hebrews 6:19-20

Cast your cares
on God;
that anchor holds.

Frank Moore Colby

The LORD is good
to those whose
hope is in Him,
to the one who
seeks Him.

Lamentations 3:25

God always
gives His best to
those who leave the
choice with Him.

Jim Elliot

May the God of hope
fill you with all joy
and peace in believing,
that you may abound
in hope by the power
of the Holy Spirit.

Romans 15:13

Hope fills the
afflicted soul with such
joy and consolation,
that it can laugh while
tears are in the eye,
sigh and sing all
in a breath.

William Gurnall

"I know the plans
I have for you,"
declares the LORD,
"plans to prosper you
and not to harm you,
plans to give you hope
and a future."

Jeremiah 29:11

God gives us
hopes and dreams
for certain things
to happen,
but He doesn't
always allow us
to see the exact
timing of His plan.

Joyce Meyer

Those who hope in the LORD will renew their strength. They will soar on wings like eagles; they will run and not grow weary, they will walk and not be faint.

Isaiah 40:31

The wings of hope
carry us, soaring
high above the
driving winds of life.

Ana Jacob

Everything that was written in the past was written to teach us, so that through endurance and encouragement we might have hope.

Romans 15:4

The word hope
I take for faith;
and indeed hope
is nothing else but
the constancy of faith.

John Calvin

Faith is confidence
in what we hope for
and assurance about
what we do not see.

Hebrews 11:1

Faith has to do with
things that are not seen
and hope with things
that are not at hand.

Thomas Aquinas

Blessed are those whose hope is in the LORD their God.

Psalm 146:5

If you have been reduced to God being your only hope, you are in a good place.

Jim Laffoon

We also glory in our sufferings, because we know that suffering produces perseverance; perseverance, character; and character, hope.

Romans 5:3-4

Only in the
darkness can you
see the stars.

Martin Luther King, Jr.

I wait for the LORD,
my whole being waits,
and in His word
I put my hope.

Psalm 130:5

Do not look to your
hope, but to Christ,
the source of your hope.

Charles H. Spurgeon

You will be secure,
because there is
hope; you will look
about you and take
your rest in safety.

Job 11:18

The safest place
in all the world is
in the will of God,
and the safest
protection in all
the world is the
name of God.

Warren Wiersbe

God will never
forget the needy;
the hope of
the afflicted
will never perish.

Psalm 9:18

If you feel like you're at the end of your rope, tie a knot and hang on! Because God's a God of miracles, and He's holding the other end.

Pat Hicks

When doubts
filled my mind,
Your comfort gave
me renewed hope
and cheer.

Psalm 94:19

Without Christ
there is no hope.

Charles H. Spurgeon

Hope does not disappoint because the love of God has been poured out in our hearts by the Holy Spirit, who was given to us.

Romans 5:5

We must accept
finite disappointment,
but never lose
infinite hope.

Martin Luther King, Jr.

Blessed is the
one who trusts
in the LORD,
whose confidence
is in Him.

Jeremiah 17:7

Positive minds full
of faith and hope
produce positive lives.

Joyce Meyer

With minds that
are alert and fully
sober, set your hope
on the grace to be
brought to you when
Jesus Christ is revealed
at His coming.

1 Peter 1:13

When God comes down, He removes the immovable difficulties. God moves on behalf of the one who waits.

Anonymous

Hope in the LORD;
for with the LORD there
is unfailing love.
His redemption
overflows.

Psalm 130:7

Other men see only
a hopeless end, but
the Christian rejoices
in an endless hope.

Gilbert M. Beeken

Hope deferred makes
the heart sick,
but a longing fulfilled
is a tree of life.

Proverbs 13:12

To live without hope
is to cease to live.

Fyodor Dostoevsky

Having been
justified by His grace
we should become
heirs according to the
hope of eternal life.

Titus 3:7

The presence
of hope in
the invincible
sovereignty of God
drives out fear.

John Piper

Now these three
remain: faith, hope
and love.

1 Corinthians 13:13

Our hope lies in
believing in God's
love for our lives.

Anonymous

My heart is glad
and my tongue
rejoices; my body also
will rest in hope.

Acts 2:26

Hope is the last
lingering light of the
human heart.
It shines when every
other is put out.

James H. Aughey

We want each
of you to show this
same diligence to the
very end, so that what
you hope for may
be fully realized.

Hebrews 6:11

Hope is the thing with feathers that perches in the soul, and sings the tune without the words, and never stops at all.

Emily Dickinson

The hopes of the godly
result in happiness.

Proverbs 10:28

Hope is one of
the principal springs
that keep mankind
in motion.

Thomas Fuller

The LORD's delight
is in those who
fear Him, those who
put their hope in His
unfailing love.

Psalm 147:11

Everything that
is done in the world
is done by hope.

Martin Luther

A better hope
is introduced,
by which we draw
near to God.

Hebrews 7:19

Great hopes make
great men.

Thomas Fuller

Let us be sober,
putting on the
breastplate of faith
and love, and as
a helmet the hope
of salvation.

1 Thessalonians 5:8

Hope is the dream
of a soul awake.

Proverb

Let us hold unswervingly to the hope we profess, for He who promised is faithful.

Hebrews 10:23

Hope is the golden thread that should be woven into every experience of life.

Anonymous

May our Lord Jesus Christ Himself and God our Father encourage your hearts and strengthen you in every good deed and word.

2 Thessalonians 2:16-17

Hope is the raw
material from which
faith builds the house.

Rex Rouis

The LORD will
be a refuge for
His people,
a stronghold
for the people.

Joel 3:16

You can have hope
without faith,
but you cannot have
faith without hope!

Randy Furco

[Love]
always protects,
always trusts,
always hopes,
always perseveres.

1 Corinthians 13:7

Optimism is the faith that leads to achievement. Nothing can be done without hope and confidence.

Helen Keller

"I am the LORD; those who hope in Me will not be disappointed."

Isaiah 49:23

If it were not for hopes,
the heart would break.

Thomas Fuller

As for me,
I will always have
hope; I will praise You
more and more.

Psalm 71:14

Let perseverance
be your engine and
hope your fuel.

H. Jackson Brown, Jr.

O Lord, You alone
are my hope.

Psalm 71:5

Hope keeps you alive.
Faith gives your life
meaning, blessings,
and a good end.

Rex Rouis

No one who
hopes in You will ever
be put to shame.

Psalm 25:3

A Christian knows
that hope is a beam
of God, a spark of glory,
and that nothing shall
extinguish it till the soul
be filled with glory.

Thomas Brooks

May integrity and uprightness protect me, because my hope, LORD, is in You.

Psalm 25:21

Hope springs eternal
in the human breast.

Alexander Pope

So, Lord, where do I put my hope? My only hope is in You.

Psalm 39:7

What gives me
the most hope is God's
grace; knowing that His
grace is going
to give me the strength
for whatever I face,
knowing that nothing
is a surprise to God.

Rick Warren

My heart is glad,
and my glory rejoices;
my flesh also will
rest in hope.

Psalm 16:9

If I do not look with eyes of hope on all in whom there is even a faint beginning, as our Lord did, then I know nothing of Calvary love.

Amy Carmichael

Why are you cast down, O my soul? Hope in God; for I shall yet praise Him, the help of my countenance and my God.

Psalm 43:5

Rejoice that the
Lord Jesus has become
your strength and your
song – He has become
your salvation.

Charles H. Spurgeon

Great peace have those who love Your law, and nothing causes them to stumble. LORD, I hope for Your salvation, and I do Your commandments.

Psalm 119:165-166

When you say that a situation or a person is hopeless, you are slamming the door in the face of God.

Charles L. Allen

I pray that the eyes
of your heart may
be enlightened in order
that you may know
the hope to which
He has called you.

Ephesians 1:18-19

Faith is the spark
that ignites the
impossible and causes
it to become possible.

Rick Renner

Wisdom is sweet to your soul. If you find it, you will have a bright future, and your hopes will not be cut short.

Proverbs 24:14

God is not a deceiver, that He should offer to support us, and then, when we lean upon Him, should slip away from us.

St. Augustine

Through our Lord Jesus Christ we have gained access by faith into this grace in which we now stand. And we boast in the hope of the glory of God.

Romans 5:2

Hope is passion
for the possible.

Søren Kierkegaard

In hope we were saved.
If we hope for what
we do not yet have,
we wait for it patiently.

Romans 8:24-25

When the world says,
"Give up," hope whispers,
"Try it one more time."

Anonymous